Word Study in Action

Words Their Way

Word Study Notebook

Donald R. Bear • Marcia Invernizzi • Francine Johnston

Contents

continued on next page

CELEBRATION PRESS
Pearson Learning Group

The following people have contributed to the development of this product:

Art and Design: John Maddalone, Liz Nemeth, Evelyn O'Shea

Editorial: Linette Mathewson

Inventory: Yvette Higgins

Marketing: Ken Clinton

Production/Manufacturing: Michele Uhl

Publishing Operations: Richetta Lobban

COVER ART: John Maddalone

ISBN 0-7652-7566-X

Printed in the United States of America
 4 5 6 7 8 9 10   09 08 07 06

Celebration Press
Pearson Learning Group

1-800-321-3106
www.pearsonlearning.com

piano	contrast	canyon
profess	react	humid
profit	tantrum	metric
season	radio	current
finance	climate	freedom
magnet	create	raisin
treaty	closet	hundred
balance	comet	transmit

Open

V/CV	VV/CV	V/V
human	reason	poet

Closed

VC/V	VC/CV	VCC/CV & VC/CCV
planet	happen	athlete/pilgrim

1. Write on the lines words that contain the following syllable junctures.
2. Draw a line between the two syllables in each word.
3. Choose two words and use each in a sentence. Write your sentences on the lines below

V/CV	VV/CV	V/V
hu/man	rea/son	po/et

VC/V	VC/CV	VCC/CV & VC/CCV
plan/et	hap/pen	ath/lete pil/grim

1. _____

_____

2. _____

_____

noted	plotted	braided
linking	solving	rated
faded	floating	grinning
cheated	proving	shouted
heating	skimming	grabbed
hiring	pacing	greeted
scanning	pointing	prompted
dozing	posing	painted

VCV	VCCV	VVCV
hoping	hopping	cleaning

1. Make new words by adding the ending -ing or -ed to the following base words. (Drop the e and double the final letter as necessary.) Write the new words on the lines.

2. Draw a line between the two syllables in each word.

3. Circle the words that contain open syllables.

-ing	-ed
link _____	note _____
pose _____	plot _____
skim _____	braid _____
float _____	fade _____
prove _____	grab _____
solve _____	shout _____
heat _____	paint _____
pace _____	quote _____
grin _____	cheat _____
hire _____	rate _____
scan _____	greet _____
doze _____	prompt _____
stand _____	clean _____
point _____	leak _____

lightning	useful	invade
debate	speaker	freezer
delete	disease	flowing
crayon	define	advice
compose	decay	refrain
remote	enclose	frighten
salute	dispute	dainty
awake	polite	brightly

Review Long Vowel Patterns in Accented Syllables

Long Vowel in 2nd Syllable

Long Vowel in 1st Syllable

1. Read each phrase. Look at the word in boldface type. Draw a line between the two syllables.
2. Circle the long vowel in each boldface word.
3. Underline the accented syllable of each boldface word.

colored **crayon**	**define** the word
invade with caution	close the **freezer**
seek **advice**	shining **brightly**
delete the mistakes	**debate** the issue
don't **frighten** animals	**useful** instructions
salute the officer	**lightning** bolt
flowing river	**remote** control
chronic **disease**	guest **speaker**
dispute the charges	**enclose** the yard
use **polite** manners	sing the **refrain**
dainty flowers	**compose** a story

Sort 3: Review Long Vowel Patterns in Accented Syllables

Review Long Vowel Pairs oa, ow, oo in Accented Syllables

goalie	boater	bloated	foamy
approach	soapy	trooper	toaster
slowly	towing	mower	afloat
below	bowling	rower	owner
gloomy	goofy	booster	poodle
baboon	lagoon	harpoon	bamboo

Sort 4: Review Long Vowel Pairs oa, ow, oo in Accented Syllables

oa	ow	oo
loafer	lower	rooster

1. Write on the lines words that contain *oa*, *ow*, and *oo*.
2. Choose three words and use each in a sentence. Write your sentences on the lines below.

oa	ow	oo
<u>loaf</u>/er	<u>low</u>/er	<u>roost</u>/er

1. _____

2. _____

3. _____

Sort 4: Review Long Vowel Pairs oa, ow, oo in Accented Syllables

Review Vowel Pairs ai, ee, ea in Accented Syllables

sustain	needle	disease	heading
feather	greatness	trainer	freezer
retreat	peasant	measure	beauty
sailor	terrain	bleachers	succeed
pleasure	captain	rainbow	refrain
reason	canteen	jealous	steady

Sort 5: Review Vowel Pairs ai, ee, ea in Accented Syllables

Review Vowel Pairs ai, ee, ea in Accented Syllables

Oddball	2ⁿᵈ Syllable Long	1ˢᵗ Syllable Short	1ˢᵗ Syllable Long

Read each of the words in the box. Write the words in the column
that shows which vowel pattern is used.

pleasure	freezer	peasant	captain	retreat	jealous	feather	sustain
disease	succeed	trainer	beauty	heading	measure	bleachers	steady
refrain	rainbow	reason	greatness	terrain	canteen	sailor	needle

1st Syllable Long

1st Syllable Short

2nd Syllable Long

Oddball

Ambiguous Vowels oy, oi, ou, ow in Accented Syllables

thousand	amount	coward	moisture
noisy	trouble	poison	avoid
double	allow	employ	annoy
about	around	county	loyal
doughnut	southern	counter	appoint
		powder	pointed

1st Syllable

oi/oy	ou/ow

2nd Syllable

oi/oy	ou/ow	Oddball

1. Write on the lines words that contain vowel patterns *oy*, *oi*, *ou*, and *ow*.
2. Circle the vowel pair within the word.
3. Choose 2 words and use each in a sentence. Write your sentences on the lines below.

oy	oi	ow = /ou/

ou	ou = ŭ	Oddball

1. _____

_____

2. _____

_____

toward	aware	parents	market
harvest	despair	haircut	carpet
barefoot	marble	repair	dairy
beware	careful	hardly	declare
fairy	pardon	barely	partner
		compare	impair

r-Influenced a in Accented Syllables

ar in 1st Syllable	ā in 1st Syllable	ā in 2nd Syllable	Oddball
garden	airplane	prepare	

1. Write on the lines words that contain the r-influenced a in the first syllable or the second syllable.
2. Choose three words and use each in a sentence. Write your sentences on the lines below.

ar in 1ˢᵗ Syllable	ā in 1ˢᵗ Syllable	ā in 2ⁿᵈ Syllable
garden	airplane	compare

1. _____

2. _____

3. _____

Sort 8: r-Influenced a in Accented Syllables

r-Influenced o in Accented Syllables

forest	sorry	record	order
ashore	normal	reward	perform
florist	explore	forty	before
adore	forward	ignore	northern
corner	chorus	inform	afford

or in 1ˢᵗ Syllable	or in 2ⁿᵈ Syllable	Oddball
morning	report	

1. Write on the lines words that contain the r-influenced o in the first syllable or the second syllable.
2. Choose three words and use each in a sentence. Write your sentences on the lines below.

or in 1ˢᵗ Syllable	or in 2ⁿᵈ Syllable	Oddball
morning	report	

1. _____

_____

2. _____

_____

3. _____

_____

wardrobe	worse	waffle
warning	world	wander
warden	worry	squat
warrior	worthy	squash
quarter	worship	squabble
quarrel	worthwhile	squad
swarm	dwarf	backward

/war/	/wor/	/wa/
warmth	worker	watch

1. Write on the lines words that contain w or the /w/ sound before the vowel.
2. Choose three words and use each in a sentence. Write your sentences on the lines below.

/war/	/wor/	/wa/
warmth	worker	watch

1. _____

2. _____

3. _____

Sort 10: Words With w or /w/ Before the Vowel

Sort
11

person	firmly	purpose
spirit	perfect	dirty
further	merry	certain
birthday	hurry	mermaid
thirsty	turtle	perhaps
birdbath	furnish	service
during	Thursday	circle

/ər/ Spelled **er**, **ir**, **ur** in First Syllables

/ər/ Spelled er, ir, ur in First Syllables

Oddball	ur	ir	er
	sturdy	thirty	nervous

Sort 11: /ər/ Spelled er, ir, ur in First Syllables

45

1. Write words that contain er, ir, and ur in the first syllable.
2. Choose three words and use each in a sentence. Write your sentences on the lines below.

er	ir	ur	Oddball
nervous	thirty	sturdy	

1. _____

2. _____

3. _____

sermon	earthquake	teardrop
sincere	cheerful	serpent
learner	spearmint	adhere
hermit	pearly	yearbook
merely	thermos	rehearse
appear	kernel	yearning
dreary	earnest	searching

/ər/ and r-Influenced e
Spelled er, ear, ere, eer in Accented Syllables

ər

er = /ur/	ear = /ur/	
mercy	early	

r-Influenced ē

ear	ere	eer
nearby	severe	career

1. Write words that contain /ər/ and r- influenced ē on the lines.
2. Choose 2 words and use each in a sentence. Write your sentences on the lines below.

ə r	
er = /ur/	**ear = /ur/**
<u>mer</u>/cy	<u>ear</u>/ly

r-Influenced ē		
ear	**ere**	**eer**
<u>near</u>/ly	se/<u>vere</u>	ca/<u>reer</u>

1. _____

_____

2. _____

_____

cradle	middle	tremble
able	table	single
settle	bottle	scribble
rifle	muscle	sample
rattle	paddle	battle
bugle	bridle	handle
cable	jungle	scramble

VCle	VCCle doublet	VCCle
title	little	simple

1. Read each sentence. Choose a word from the box that best completes the sentence and write it on the line. (Note: Not all words have to be used and each word can be used only once.)
2. Draw a line between the two syllables in each word.
3. Underline the accented syllable of each word.

scramble	battle	cable	rattle	scribble	able	rifle
handle	tremble	settle	cradle	bugle	jungle	single
table	paddle	bridle	middle	muscle	sample	bottle

1. The kayaker used her _____ to glide across the water.

2. Amin's family eats dinner at the _____ each night.

3. Megan's hands _____ when she is nervous.

4. The audience heard the _____ blare at the concert.

5. The athlete pulled a _____ while running.

6. The veterinarian used his hands to _____ the kitten.

7. Sonya ordered a _____ of water with lunch.

8. Monkeys and tigers live in the _____ .

9. The rock climber used a safety _____ when climbing.

Sort 13: Unaccented Final Syllable -le

saddle	level	April
total	fragile	couple
angel	fossil	metal
special	angle	novel
evil	signal	needle
pedal	stencil	local
bundle	vowel	journal
cancel	pupil	jewel
struggle	council	

Unaccented Final Syllable /əl/ Spelled -le, -el, -il, -al

-le	-el	-il	-al	Oddball
cattle	model	pencil	final	

1. Write on the lines words that contain -le, -el, -il, or -al in the final syllable.

2. Underline the accented syllable of each word.

-le cattle	-el model	-il pencil	-al final	Oddball

Sort 14: Unaccented Final Syllable /əl/ Spelled -le, -el, -il, -al

brother	doctor	dollar
favor	rather	solar
cover	flavor	mirror
motor	sugar	grammar
weather	silver	father
rumor	popular	tractor
mother	harbor	lunar
regular	cedar	after
calendar	flower	error

-er	-ar	-or
spider	collar	color

1. Write on the lines words that contain -er, -ar, or -or in the final syllable.
2. Draw a line between the two syllables and underline the accented syllable in each word.
3. Choose three words and use each in a sentence. Write your sentences on the lines below.

-er	-ar	-or
<u>spi</u>/der	<u>col</u>/lar	<u>col</u>/or

1. _____

_____

2. _____

_____

3. _____

_____

dreamer	creator	later
sooner	driver	sailor
stronger	farmer	visitor
smaller	jogger	editor
fresher	writer	younger
swimmer	older	smoother
voter	director	juror
governor	shopper	brighter

People Who Do Things		Words to Compare
dancer	actor	bigger

1. Read each word. Make new words by adding the ending -er, -ar, or -or. (Double the final consonant and drop the e as necessary.) Write the new words on the lines.

2. Write an A above the agents and a C above the comparatives.

Agent or Comparative	Agent or Comparative
shop _____	edit _____
old _____	write _____
dream _____	strong _____
create _____	young _____
big _____	vote _____
drive _____	smooth _____
visit _____	sail _____
soon _____	farm _____
jog _____	govern _____
fresh _____	swim _____
dance _____	small _____
direct _____	act _____
bright _____	jury _____

rancher	nature	pressure
failure	senior	teacher
capture	pleasure	danger
pitcher	future	leisure
mixture	treasure	pasture
culture	posture	obscure
secure	stretcher	marcher
torture		

More Final Syllables /ər/ Spelled -cher, -ture, -sure, -ure

-cher = /chur/	-ture = /chur/	-sure = /zhur/	-ure = /yur/	Oddball
catcher	picture	measure	figure	

Sort 17: More Final Syllables /ər/ Spelled -cher, -ture, -sure, -ure

69

Write on the lines words that contain -cher, -ture, -sure, or -ure in the final syllable.

-cher = /chur/	-ture = /chur/
catcher	picture

-sure = /zhur/	-ure = /yur/	Oddball
measure	figure	

Sort 17: More Final Syllables /ər/ Spelled -cher, -ture, -sure, -ure

eleven	unison	captain
woman	mission	oxygen
gallon	bargain	organ
heaven	ribbon	fountain
orphan	chosen	apron
curtain	slogan	abdomen
bacon	children	certain
urban	pardon	villain

Unaccented Final Syllable /ən/ Spelled -en, -on, -an, -ain

-en	-on	-an	-ain	Oddball
broken	dragon	human	mountain	

1. Read the beginning of each word. Choose the final syllable
   -en, -on, -an, or -ain that best completes the word.
2. Write the new word on the line and read it aloud.
3. Choose three words and use each in a sentence. Write your sentences
   on the lines below.

elev____ _____	fount____ _____
suburb____ _____	heav____ _____
capt____ _____	ribb____ _____
wom____ _____	chos____ _____
oxyg____ _____	orph____ _____
missi____ _____	apr____ _____
gall____ _____	curt____ _____
barg____ _____	slog____ _____
org____ _____	childr____ _____
abdom____ _____	bac____ _____
urb____ _____	pard____ _____
unis____ _____	cert____ _____
vill____ _____	

1. _____

_____

2. _____

_____

3. _____

_____

another	degree	believe
divide	awhile	depend
between	direct	among
desire	beneath	upon
aboard	develop	because
against	defend	begun
afraid	aloud	astonish
behavior	agenda	decision
beforehand	delete	

Unaccented Initial Syllables a-, de-, be-

a-	de-	be-	Oddball
again	debate	beyond	

1. Read the ending of each word. Choose the initial syllable a-, de-, or be- that best completes the word.
2. Write the new word on the line and read it aloud.
3. Choose two words and use each in a sentence. Write your sentences on the lines below.

___nother _____

___gree _____

___lieve _____

___stonish _____

___while _____

___yond _____

___pend _____

___tween _____

___mong _____

___sire _____

___gain _____

___genda _____

___forehand _____

___neath _____

___board _____

___velop _____

___cause _____

___gainst _____

___fend _____

___gun _____

___bate _____

___fraid _____

___loud _____

___lete _____

___havior _____

___cision _____

1. _____

_____

2. _____

_____

circle	gymnast	common
gossip	central	giraffe
camel	golden	century
genius	college	garage
cyclist	general	custom
gutter	cider	gingerbread
collect	cereal	govern
gurgle	cavern	giant

Initial Hard and Soft c and g

Hard g	Hard c	Soft g	Soft c
gather	correct	gentle	cement

1. Read each sentence. Choose a word from the box that best completes the sentence and write it on the line. (Note: Not all words will be used and each word can be used only once.)
2. Underline the vowel that follows the c or g.
3. Circle the word if it has a soft c or g.

circle	central	century	cyclist	cider	gather
gymnast	giraffe	genius	govern	giant	correct
common	cavern	college	custom	collect	cement
gossip	golden	garage	gutter	cereal	gentle

1. The book club will _____ weekly.

2. The _____ gained speed on the downhill slope.

3. Aida plans to major in biology at _____.

4. The teacher outlined the _____ concept of the project.

5. The craftsman made a _____ desk.

6. My cousin is training to become a _____.

7. Apple _____ was served at the harvest party.

8. Some of the leaves had changed to a _____ color.

9. Malik volunteered to _____ the problem.

10. There was a _____ breeze near the ocean.

11. The class measured the diameter of the _____.

12. Cheryl stores her athletic equipment in the _____.

13. We explored the underground _____.

14. Our teacher asked for a volunteer to _____ our reports.

15. My teacher discourages _____ at school.

garbage	police	manage	midget
princess	gadget	sentence	actress
luggage	address	surgeon	distance
science	package	compass	office
courage	message	practice	village
express	possess	challenge	arrange

Final -s and Soft c and g

-age = /ij/ bandage									

ge = /j/ budget									

-ss = /s/ recess									

-ce = /s/ notice									

Write on the lines words that contain -ce, -ss, ge, or -age in the final syllable.

-ce = /s/ notice	-ss = /s/ recess	-ge = /j/ budget	-age = /ij/ bandage

vague	guard	language
gauge	shrug	league
guitar	zigzag	guide
fatigue	iceberg	argue
strong	guilty	guest
dialog	guidance	plague
intrigue	catalog	penguin

More Words With g

Oddball	-g ladybug	-gue tongue	gu- guess

Read each sentence. Choose a word from the box that best completes the sentences and write it on the line. (Note: Not all words will be used and each word can be used only once.)

guard	guitar	guide	guilty	guidance
vague	league	fatigue	strong	plague
zigzag	shrug	iceberg	guest	intrigue
gauge	language	argue	dialog	catalog

1. The musician played a _____ while she sang.

2. My grandfather has a _____ memory of his childhood.

3. Claire picked out a new outfit from the _____.

4. The coach encouraged the players to _____ off their loss.

5. Jin planned his class schedule with some _____ from his advisor.

6. The smell of the fresh flowers was _____.

7. The bowling _____ competes on Saturday mornings.

8. Tourists followed a tour _____ around the city.

9. My grandmother speaks more than one _____.

10. The actor memorized his _____ for the movie.

11. After the marathon, Marcella was overcome with _____.

12. The hikers followed the _____ path down the mountain.

13. We went to the auditorium to hear the _____ speaker.

14. The penguins gathered on the _____.

15. A light went on when the gas _____ was near empty.

quick	pocket	traffic
index	stomach	hammock
nickel	topic	complex
attack	pickle	picnic
buckle	metric	ticket
electric	plastic	perplex
shoebox	jacket	racetrack
rocket	fabric	unlock
struck	specific	

/k/ Spelled ck, -ic, -x

-ck	ck	-ic	-x	Oddball
shock	chicken	magic	relax	

Write on the lines words that contain the /k/ sound spelled as ck, -ic, or -x.

-ck shock	ck chicken	-ic magic

-x relax	Oddball

Sort 23: /k/ Spelled ck, -ic, -x

/qw/ and /k/ Spelled qu

squirrel	racquet	frequent
equator	squirming	mosquito
quotation	banquet	quadrant
queasy	liquid	quizzes
qualify	request	sequel
		critique

quality
equipment
conquer
inquire
sequence
technique

1st Syllable	2nd Syllable	qu = /k/
question	equal	antique

1. Read each sentence. Choose a word from the box that best completes the sentence and write it on the line. (Note: Not all words will be used and each word can be used only once.)
2. Draw a line between the two syllables in each word.

request	quality	sequel	conquer	inquire	queasy
question	frequent	mosquito	equator	quizzes	sequence
equal	racquet	squirming	banquet	liquid	qualify
antique	equipment	squirrel	quotation	technique	quadrant

1. The tennis player prepared to serve by raising his _____.

2. Snowstorms in the northeast are _____ in winter.

3. Shayna located the _____ on the globe.

4. My grandmother has several _____ quilts in her home.

5. Some of the kids felt _____ after the roller-coaster ride.

6. My sister hopes to _____ for the race.

7. The coach spoke at the awards _____.

8. The _____ buried the acorns in the yard.

9. Luckily, I returned from the forest with no _____ bites.

10. My backpack is made of _____ material.

11. The team hoped to _____ its opponent.

12. The hiker was responsible for carrying her _____ on the expedition.

13. Raj called the radio station with his music _____.

14. Our English teacher likes to give surprise _____.

15. Vonelle could not wait to read the _____ to the novel.

fasten	resign	wreckage
knowledge	honor	thought
listen	assignment	wrestle
rhyme	brought	glisten
answer	rhythm	bought
khaki	though	doorknob
campaign	kneepad	soften
gnarl	sword	knockout

Silent t castle	Silent g design	Silent w wrinkle

Silent k knuckle	Silent h honest	Silent gh through

1. Read the incomplete word. Choose the silent letter t, g, w, k, h, or letters gh that best completes the word.
2. Write the new word on the line and read it aloud.
3. Choose three words and use each in a sentence. Write your sentences on the lines below.

fas___en _____

___nowledge _____

lis___en _____

r___yme _____

ans___er _____

campai___n _____

___narl _____

k___aki _____

resi___n _____

___onor _____

assi___nment _____

brou___t _____

r___ythm _____

thou___ _____

___neepad _____

s___ord _____

___reckage _____

thou___t _____

___restle _____

glis___en _____

bou___t _____

door___nob _____

sof___en _____

___knockout _____

physics	elephant	cough
naughty	phantom	nephew
tough	taught	photocopy
dolphin	rough	caught
photograph	trophy	laughter
fought	telephone	homophone
paragraph	phonics	height

Words With gh and ph

Silent gh	-gh = /f/	ph	ph-
daughter	enough	alphabet	phrase

1. Write words on the lines that contain ph, gh = /f/, and silent gh.

2. Choose three words and use each in a sentence. Write your sentences on the lines below.

ph- phrase	ph alphabet	-gh = /f/ enough	silent gh daughter

1. _____

2. _____

3. _____

1. _____

2. _____

3. _____

recopy	uncle	unkind
recycle	unwrap	reptile
refill	unselfish	refinish
unbutton	unhappy	rewrite
retrace	unpack	retake
unfair	return	uneven
review	unequal	unbeaten
remodel	rescue	

Prefixes re-, un-

re-	un-	Oddball
rebuild	unable	

1. Write the meaning of the prefix on the line next to each header.

Prefix re-: _____

Prefix un-: _____

2. Make new words by adding the prefix re- or un- to the
   following base words. Write the words on the lines.
   (Note: You can add more than one prefix to some words.)

___build _____   ___button _____

___able _____   ___write _____

___copy _____   ___trace _____

___cycle _____   ___pack _____

___kind _____   ___take _____

___wrap _____   ___fair _____

___fill _____   ___turn _____

___selfish _____   ___even _____

___finish _____   ___view _____

___happy _____   ___equal _____

___model _____   ___beaten _____

dislike	mistreat	prefix
precious	disable	mismatch
premature	disobey	misplace
preteen	displace	misbehave
preview	dishonest	misjudge
preheat	disloyal	pretest
disappear	precaution	mister
miscount	distant	mistrust

Prefixes dis-, mis-, pre-

dis-	mis-	pre-	Oddball
disagree	misspell	preschool	

1. Make new words by adding the prefix dis-, mis-, or pre- to the following base words. Write the words on the lines. (Note: You can add more than one prefix to some words.)

___like _____

___treat _____

___fix _____

___able _____

___match _____

___mature _____

___obey _____

___place _____

___teen _____

___cover _____

___spell _____

___count _____

___behave _____

___view _____

___honest _____

___judge _____

___heat _____

___loyal _____

___test _____

___appear _____

___caution _____

___agree _____

___school _____

___trust _____

2. Choose three derived words and write a definition for each.

1. _____

2. _____

3. _____

extend	nonfiction	incorrect
forearm	extra	nonstop
indecent	forehead	express
nonfat	foresee	exclude
foreshadow	explode	income
foremost	expand	nonprofit
insight	explore	indoor
nonskid	inhuman	

Prefixes ex-, non-, in-, fore-

fore-	in- ("not")	non-	ex-
forecast	incomplete	nonsense	exit
	in- ("in" or "into")		
	indent		

1. Write the meaning of the prefix on the line next to each header.

Prefix ex-: _____

Prefix non-: _____

Prefix in-: _____

Prefix fore-: _____

2. Make new words by adding the prefix ex-, non-, in-, or fore- to the following base words or word parts. Write the words on the lines. (Note: You can add more than one prefix to some words.)

___tend _____

___fiction _____

___correct _____

___arm _____

___plore _____

___stop _____

___decent _____

___head _____

___press _____

___fat _____

___see _____

___clude _____

___profit _____

___shadow _____

___plode _____

___come _____

___most _____

___pand _____

___door _____

___sight _____

___human _____

___complete _____

___sense _____

___cast _____

___dent _____

___skid _____

Prefixes uni-, bi-, tri-, and Other Numbers

unique	unity	biweekly	trilogy
octagon	bisect	triangle	unicorn
octopus	triple	bilingual	pentagon
unison	October	triplet	union
universe	trio	uniform	tripod

Prefixes uni-, bi-, tri-, and Other Numbers

uni-	bi-	tri-	Other Number Prefix
unicycle	bicycle	tricycle	quadrangle

1. Write the meaning of the prefix on the line next to each header.

Prefix uni-: _____

Prefix bi-: _____

Prefix tri-: _____

Other Number Prefix: _____

2. Make new words by adding the prefix uni-, bi-, tri-, or that of some other number to the following base words or word parts. Write the words on the lines. (Note: You can add more than one prefix to some words or word parts.)

___cycle _____

___rangle _____

___ty _____

___weekly _____

___logy _____

___agon _____

___corn _____

___sect _____

___angle _____

___que _____

___lingual _____

___ple _____

___opus _____

___on _____

___plet _____

___ober _____

___son _____

___pod _____

___form _____

___verse _____

clearly	quickly	easily
angrily	rainy	foggy
snowy	noisily	lazily
loudly	quietly	dimly
stormy	misty	windy
daily	cloudy	roughly
chilly	sleepily	breezy
busily	smoothly	merrily

-y	-ly	-ily
sunny	slowly	happily

1. Read each sentence. Choose a base word from the box that best completes the sentence. (Note: Not all words will be used and each word can be used only once.)

2. Add the suffix -y, -ly, or -ily to the word. (Change -y to i, drop the e, and double the final letter as necessary.) Write the adjective or adverb on the line.

rain	clear	lazy	storm	cloud	breeze	merry
quick	angry	mist	loud	rough	happy	sleepy
easy	snow	quiet	chill	wind	sun	busy
fog	dim	noisy	day	smooth	slow	

1. During _____ weather, we prepare to stay indoors.

2. The emergency vehicle moved _____ to the hospital.

3. After much practice, Dana _____ completed the equation.

4. We used a flashlight to explore the _____ lit cave.

5. My family likes to ski in a _____ location.

6. Our cat _____ moved from the floor after napping.

7. The news anchor _____ delivered his lines.

8. Greg _____ shared his good news with the class.

9. At the library, we work together _____.

10. The excited friends _____ greeted one another.

11. Flying a kite is fun to do on a _____ day.

12. Talia shielded her face from the _____ wind.

13. The parade of people passed _____ through town.

14. The hikers moved slowly up the _____ path.

15. On _____ days it's fun to look for shapes in the sky.

calmer	prettiest	dirtier
easiest	closer	crazier
coolest	calmest	hotter
fewest	closest	craziest
weaker	prettier	easier
dirtiest	fewer	hottest
cooler	weakest	lazier
funniest	laziest	funnier

Comparatives -er, -est

-er							
braver							

-est							
bravest							

-ier							
happier							

-iest							
happiest							

1. Make new words by adding the suffix -er or -est to the following base words. (Change -y to i, drop the e, and double the final letter as necessary.) Write the words on the lines.

2. Write three new base words on the lines provided. Make new words by adding the suffix -er or -est to these words. (Change -y to i, drop the e, and double the final letter as necessary.) Write the words on the lines.

	-er	-est
funny	_____	_____
lazy	_____	_____
calm	_____	_____
easy	_____	_____
close	_____	_____
pretty	_____	_____
few	_____	_____
crazy	_____	_____
cool	_____	_____
dirty	_____	_____
hot	_____	_____
weak	_____	_____
brave	_____	_____
happy	_____	_____
_____	_____	_____
_____	_____	_____
_____	_____	_____

Suffixes -ness, -ful, -less

colorful	goodness	thankfulness
thoughtfulness	faithful	helplessness
illness	weakness	peacefulness
kindness	painful	worthless
fearful	harmless	plentiful
truthfulness	awareness	fearless
	hopeless	
	happiness	
	restless	
	penniless	
	dreadful	
	gratefulness	

Suffixes -ness, -ful, -less

Combination of Suffixes	-less	-ful	-ness
carelessness	homeless	graceful	darkness

1. Write the meaning of the suffix on the line next to each header.

Suffix -ness: _____

Suffix -ful: _____

Suffix -less: _____

2. Make new words by adding the suffix -ness, -ful, or -less, or a combination of these suffixes to the following base words. (Change -y to i as necessary.) Write the words on the lines.

care	_____	ill	_____
home	_____	thought	_____
dark	_____	rest	_____
grace	_____	peace	_____
good	_____	kind	_____
color	_____	hope	_____
hope	_____	pain	_____
thank	_____	penny	_____
weak	_____	happy	_____
faith	_____	fear	_____
worth	_____	harm	_____
help	_____	plenty	_____
dread	_____	truth	_____
aware	_____	grate	_____

cellar	weather
allowed	flour
bored	seller
whether	aloud
flower	board
vary	their
desert	principle
chews	merry
very	higher
dessert	principal
choose	marry
there	hire

berry	bury

1. Say each word aloud. Think of a word that sounds the same but is spelled differently and has a different meaning.
2. Write a sentence that uses the new word.
3. Underline the homophone.

cellar _____

weather _____

allowed _____

flower _____

board _____

their _____

merry _____

very _____

dessert _____

principal _____

choose _____

hire _____

bury _____

desert _____

aloud _____

present	**des**ert
record	**per**mit
rebel	**ob**ject
subject	**re**ject
produce	**con**duct
export	**con**tract
pres**ent**	des**ert**
re**cord**	per**mit**
re**bel**	ob**ject**
sub**ject**	re**ject**
pro**duce**	con**duct**
ex**port**	con**tract**

Noun	Verb

1. Try saying each word two ways by changing the accented syllable.
2. Write a sentence that uses the word.
3. Underline the accented syllable of each homograph.

record _____

present _____

desert _____

permit _____

rebel _____

object _____

subject _____

reject _____

produce _____

conduct _____

export _____

contract _____

Sort 35: Homographs

Vowel Pairs ie, ei

eighteen	ceiling	weird	niece
deceive	either	grief	mischief
conceited	neither	shield	weigh
freight	receipt	relieve	sleigh
protein	belief	reign	yield
vein	beige	perceive	leisure

Vowel Pairs ie, ei

ie = ē	ei = ē	ei = ā	cei = ē	
thief	seize	neighbor	receive	
			Oddball	

1. Read the incomplete word. Choose the vowel pair *ie* or *ei* that completes the word. (Remember the rule "*i* before *e* except after *c*.") Write the new word on the line.

2. Read the words aloud.

3. Circle the words that contain long *a*.

n__ce	sl__gh
w__rd	rel__ve
c__ling	rec__pt
__ghteen	fr__ght
misch__f	y__ld
gr__f	r__gn
__ther	bel__f
dec__ve	th__f
w__gh	s__ze
sh__ld	n__ghbor
n__ther	rec__ve
conc__t	perc__ve
v__n	l__sure
prot__n	b__ge

Listen to each word as it is read aloud. Write the word in the box that shows its correct vowel pattern.

VCV	VVCV
_____	_____
_____	_____
_____	_____
_____	_____
_____	_____

VCCV	VCCCV
_____	_____
_____	_____
_____	_____
_____	_____
_____	_____

Listen to each word as it is read aloud. Write the word in the box that shows its correct placement of the long vowel pattern.

Long Vowel in 1ˢᵗ Syllable	Long Vowel in 2ⁿᵈ Syllable

Listen to each word as it is read aloud. Write the word in the box that shows its correct ambiguous vowel pattern.

SPELL CHECK 2a

oy/oi	ou/ow	au

aw	al

Listen to each word as it is read aloud. Write the word in the box that shows its correct r-influenced vowel pattern.

ar	are	air

or	ore

Listen to each word as it is read aloud. Write the word in the box that shows its correct /ər/ and r-influenced vowel spelling.

er	ir	ur

ear = /ur/	r-Influenced ē ear/ere/eer

Listen to each word as it is read aloud. Write the words on the lines.

1. _____

2. _____

3. _____

4. _____

5. _____

6. _____

7. _____

8. _____

9. _____

10. _____

11. _____

12. _____

13. _____

14. _____

15. _____

16. _____

17. _____

18. _____

19. _____

20. _____

21. _____

22. _____

23. _____

24. _____

Listen to each word as it is read aloud. Write the word in the box that shows its r-influenced vowel pattern.

-er spider	-or color	-ar collar

Listen to each word as it is read aloud. Write the word in the box that shows its correct final or initial syllable.

a-	de-	be-

/ər/	/ən/

Listen to each word as it is read aloud. Write the word in the box that shows its correct consonant sound.

Hard c	Hard g
_____	_____
_____	_____
_____	_____
_____	_____
_____	_____
_____	_____

Soft c	Soft g	Final s
_____	_____	_____
_____	_____	_____
_____	_____	_____
_____	_____	_____
_____	_____	_____
_____	_____	_____

Listen to each word as it is read aloud. Write the words on the lines.

1. _____

2. _____

3. _____

4. _____

5. _____

6. _____

7. _____

8. _____

9. _____

10. _____

11. _____

12. _____

13. _____

14. _____

15. _____

16. _____

17. _____

18. _____

19. _____

20. _____

21. _____

22. _____

23. _____

24. _____

SPELL CHECK 5

1. Listen to each word as it is read aloud. Write the word on the line.
2. Write a definition for the word.
3. Write a sentence using the word.
4. In the space provided, draw a picture that connects to the word.

Spell: _____

Define: _____

Sentence: _____

Spell: _____

Define: _____

Sentence: _____

Listen to each word as it is read aloud. Write the word on the line in the first column. Then add at least one ending to the base word and write the new word in the correct column.

SPELL CHECK 6

Base Word

1. _____
2. _____
3. _____
4. _____
5. _____
6. _____
7. _____
8. _____
9. _____
10. _____
11. _____
12. _____
13. _____
14. _____
15. _____

Add -y, -ly, -ily

1. _____
2. _____
3. _____
4. _____
5. _____
6. _____
7. _____
8. _____
9. _____
10. _____
11. _____
12. _____
13. _____
14. _____
15. _____

Add -er, -est

1. _____
2. _____
3. _____
4. _____
5. _____
6. _____
7. _____
8. _____
9. _____
10. _____
11. _____
12. _____
13. _____
14. _____
15. _____

Add -ness, -ful, -less

1. _____
2. _____
3. _____
4. _____
5. _____
6. _____
7. _____
8. _____
9. _____
10. _____
11. _____
12. _____
13. _____
14. _____
15. _____

1. Listen to each word as it is read aloud. Write the word on the line in the first column.

2. Write a homophone or homograph for each word.

3. Underline the accented syllable in each homograph.

SPELL CHECK 7a

1. _____
2. _____
3. _____
4. _____
5. _____
6. _____
7. _____
8. _____
9. _____
10. _____
11. _____
12. _____
13. _____
14. _____
15. _____

1. _____
2. _____
3. _____
4. _____
5. _____
6. _____
7. _____
8. _____
9. _____
10. _____
11. _____
12. _____
13. _____
14. _____
15. _____

4. Use several of the above words in a meaningful sentence.

_____

_____

Listen to each word as it is read aloud. Write each word on the lines below.

1. _____

2. _____

3. _____

4. _____

5. _____

6. _____

7. _____

8. _____

9. _____

10. _____

11. _____

12. _____

13. _____

14. _____

15. _____

16. _____

17. _____

18. _____

Choose two words from your list and use them in a sentence.

_____

_____

Spell Check 7b: Vowel Patterns ie, ei